Old MOTHERWELL and NEWARTF

by
Oliver van Helden

Merry Street looking towards the cross, with the entrance to Brandon Street on the left beyond the Motherwell Inn.

© Oliver van Helden 2000
First published in the United Kingdom, 2000,
by Stenlake Publishing
Telephone / Fax: 01290 551122
Reprinted 2006
Printed in Great Britain by St. Edmundsbury Press Ltd

ISBN 1 84033 106 2

ACKNOWLEDGEMENTS

I would like to thank the following people for their help with this book: Robert Grieves for providing the pictures that appear on page 6 and the inside back cover, plus supplementary information on buses and bus services. John McKillop for the picture of Ravenscraig on the inside front cover. Alastair White for permission to use the picture on page 22. Ronnie and Alexis MacLeod and Archie Tulloch for providing additional information about Newarthill's history. The staff of Motherwell Heritage Centre's local history lab.

Special thanks are due to the Rev. J. B. Allan for his help in identifying pictures, and for introducing me to Ian and Mima Aitken, who located the picture on page 7, and gave me additional information on many of the pictures of Motherwell.

FURTHER READING

The books listed below were used by the author during his research. None of them are available from Stenlake Publishing. Those interested in finding out more are advised to contact their local bookshop or reference library.

Clarke's Motherwell Directory, 1896.
Historic and Descriptive Sketches of the Joint Burgh of Motherwell & Wishaw and Surrounding District, T. Orr, 1925.
Historic Buildings in Motherwell District, Motherwell District Council Department of Planning, 1981.
Iron and Steel Works of the World, Metal Bulletin Books Ltd., 1991.
Lanarkshire Tramways, Ian L. Cormack, The Scottish Tramway Museum Society, c.1971.
Motherwell Memories, T. Johnstone, Hamilton Advertiser, 1938.
The Newarthill Story (three different editions), Newarthill History Group.
Ordnance Gazetteer of Scotland, ed. F. H. Groome, Thomas C. Jack, 1886.
Statistical Account of Scotland, 1792
New Statistical Account of Scotland, 1836.
Third Statistical Account of Scotland, 1960.
Steel and Steelworkers, The Sons of Vulcan, Charles Docherty, Heinemann Educational Books, 1983.
The Steel Industry in Post War Britain, David W. Heal, David & Charles, 1974.
Steelopolis, The Making of Motherwell c.1750-1939, Robert Duncan, Motherwell District Council, 1991.
Motherwell Times, various dates.
Motherwell Standard, 1905.

INTRODUCTION

Despite its size, Motherwell is a relatively modern town, and didn't exist – even as a village – before the beginning of the nineteenth century. At the 1801 census the population of Dalziel Parish numbered only 611 souls, making up a scattered community consisting largely of tenant farmers and handloom weavers. The Rev. Robert Clason, who wrote the *Statistical Account* for the parish in 1792, described exactly how far-flung the population was: 'In two places only there are clusters [of cottages] nearby together, which may be called small villages, there being 15 houses in the one, and 12 in the other'. He added that 'the condition of the tenants, with their moderate farms, and plain manner of life, is perhaps as happy as any to be met with'.

Nevertheless, there was evidence that life in rural Lanarkshire was becoming more sophisticated. Of the women in Dalziel Parish Clason wrote: 'The greatest luxury which prevails among them, is drinking tea and smoking tobacco, in which they all indulge. Their dress is also more showy and expensive than formerly'. These social trends reflected gradually increasing prosperity, which was partly brought about by agricultural improvements. The simplest techniques, such as planting hedges and trees to provide shelter for crops, were novel at the time, but contributed to increased yields and more dependable harvests. Crop rotation was a means of increasing the fertility of the soil. Handloom weaving also became more lucrative, with Clason noting that: 'of late the young girls belonging to the cottages have learned to flower muslin, in large frames made for the purpose, which they find more profitable [than spinning yarn]'.

Even though its economy was almost entirely based on agriculture, there were suggestions that Dalziel could develop different resources in the future. Two important turnpike roads traversed the parish, one linking Glasgow and Lanark, the other Edinburgh and Hamilton. The presence of mineral deposits was noted by Clason, who observed that: 'Large beds of excellent pit coal have been found in this parish . . . but none of them are wrought at present, as coal is cheap and plenty in the neighbourhood.' These abundant reserves, combined with proximity to Glasgow and a means of getting to and from the city, were the foundations on which Motherwell was built.

By the time the Rev. James Clason (Robert's son) wrote the *New Statistical Account* for Dalziel in 1836, the population was becoming consolidated in distinct communities. He recorded that 'There are three villages in the parish, viz. Motherwell', containing 'about one-half of the population of the parish', Windmillhill, 'close to the church', and Craigneuk 'half a-mile to the east'.

Forestry was important at the time, with 410 of the '1873 arable acres Scotch' of the parish covered by planted woodland; a significant 22%. Clason also talks at length about fruit-growing, writing: 'There is no situation on the Clyde more favourable for the cultivation of orchards than this parish, – very few spots, indeed, equal'. He put this down to 'The soil and climate being inland, and consequently free from the blasting influence of mildews and fogs'. The orchards occupied between 45 and 50 acres of the parish, with apples, pears and 'plumbs' the most commonly cultivated fruit. Clason lists 25 varieties of apples, including Dalzell Manse Codlin, Red Colville and Cambusnethan Pippin.

Again, coal is referred to incidentally, with the minister noting that it 'abounds in this parish, but it is only wrought at No. 1 or Engine Pit, near Coursington'. Increases in the population over the previous sixty years are described as 'chiefly owing to the improvements in the cotton and silk manufactures', and Clason's record of the employment of his parishioners provides an insight into the relative importance of different occupations: 'families employed in agriculture, 46; persons employed in manufactures [i.e. weaving], 205; labourers in mines, 18; persons employed in handicraft, masons, 13; wrights, 9; shoemakers, 9; smiths, 20; tailors, 6'. Talk of the new railway is couched in terms of its potential advantages to agriculture and quarrying, with no mention of coal: 'Lime is much wanted for the land in this parish. . . . But should the Wishaw and Coltness railway be carried forward, of which there is now a fair prospect, lime and manure of all kinds will be rendered more accessible, or rather more easily obtained.'

The Wishaw and Coltness Railway was, however, conceived 'to convey the mineral treasures of the parishes of Cambusnethan, Dalziel, Bothwell, and Old Monkland, to Glasgow' (*Historic Sketches*), and when it opened in 1841 it formed the first stage of an extensive transport network that quickly connected Motherwell with the rest of Britain. The first stretch of the railway, operational in the early 1830s, was 'worked by horse power' – i.e. horses were harnessed to the carriages and towed them along the tracks – but locomotive power was introduced soon after. Between July 1842 and December 1844 the Wishaw and Coltness Railway carried 117,413 passengers and over 1.1 million tons of goods. In 1848 the line became part of a major national route owned by the Caledonian Railway, and they built a station on a site off Brandon Street (although the street probably didn't have a name at that time), in what later became Melville Drive.

The population of Dalziel Parish grew dramatically following the arrival of the railway, rising from 2,262 in 1851 to 9,175 in 1871, with the burgeoning village of Motherwell the focal point for this growth. In 1845 the West of Scotland Malleable Iron Company established an ironworks next to the village. This was purchased by the Glasgow Iron Company in 1853, and they operated it successfully for over 50 years. In April 1865, a group of Motherwell residents presented a petition 'To declare the locality a populous place in terms of the [Police] Act [1862] and define its boundaries' (*Historic Sketches*). Despite being called a Police Act, this was concerned with the infrastructure of the town, and made provisions for local government and improvements to utilities. Providing an adequate water supply and proper sanitation were important issues for Motherwell's new commissioners.

David Colville established the Dalzell Iron Works in 1871, and these converted to steel production about a decade later. A gazetteer of Scotland, published in 1896, stated that: 'The malleable iron-works of the Glasgow Iron Company are the largest in Scotland, with 50 puddling furnaces and 8 rolling mills; and Mr D. Colville's steel-works, where operations were commenced on 20 Oct. 1880, now employs over 1000 men'. The Lanarkshire Steel Company's works were officially opened in March 1891, by which time Motherwell had become irrevocably associated with steel-making.

With the establishment of these new works – which consumed locally-mined coal and ironstone, and used the railway network to distribute their products – Motherwell's growth became unstoppable. Expert and unskilled workers were brought in from wherever they could be had, houses were built hastily by the employers who required a workforce, and over a short period of time the former village acquired the trappings of a Victorian industrial town. In August 1885, the *Motherwell Times* described the changes that had been seen since the arrival of the railway in 1841: 'What was then woods and fields has been covered with houses and works, which darken the air with smoke, and give the streets quite a Glasgowegian [*sic*] aspect'.

The Dalzell works and Lanarkshire Steel Co. were merged as Colvilles in 1936, and in 1952 employed 5,460 people between the two sites. However, in the second half of the twentieth century heavy industry in Motherwell went into decline. This reflected an internationally-changing market place and the depletion of local mineral reserves. Ironically, Motherwell's most famous steelworks was built during this period of decline, and the closure of Ravenscraig in 1992 had a devastating impact on the town, particularly because of the huge numbers of workers who were made redundant. Nonetheless, Motherwell is still home to Dalzell steelworks, while companies such as Motherwell Bridge perpetuate the town's heavy industrial past.

Like Motherwell, Newarthill owed its prosperity and growth to the mineral reserves around it. Because coal lay closer to the surface in the Newarthill and Carfin areas, it was exploited on a large scale at a much earlier date than in Motherwell. As a result Newarthill was well-established at a time when Motherwell was still a small village. However, the coal seams had been largely worked out by the 1920s, and a large proportion of the population of Newarthill subsequently found work in Motherwell. Latterly the industrial estates at Carfin and Newhouse became the focus for local employment.

Motherwell has survived the closure of Ravenscraig, and is a bustling and lively town. Excellent transport links were one of the factors that led to it becoming an industrial centre, and Motherwell still has these, with the M74 nearby, and a station on the west coast main line making Glasgow and the rest of the UK easily and quickly accessible. Many of the environmental scars left behind by the erstwhile pits and works have been healed, and the town continues to prosper.

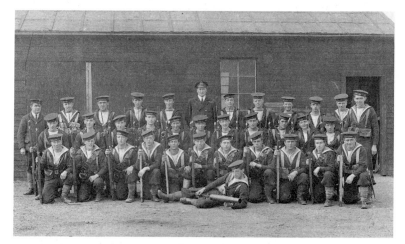

The message on the back of this postcard reads 'Naval Guard at the Clyde Valley Electrical Power Station, Motherwell, Scotland. July 5th 1921.' Unfortunately the edition of the *Motherwell Times* for this date is one of the few copies not on microfilm, and no information on the event has been unearthed elsewhere.

The old Clyde Bridge was designed by James Watt and is believed to have been built in 1770. In March 1782 flooding caused the river to rise almost two feet higher than ever previously known, with the water reaching sixteen feet above its normal level. Another flood in autumn 1807 washed away the two central arches of the bridge, and in February 1920 traffic was prevented from travelling across it because floods had submerged the roadway. When a new bridge was being discussed in the 1920s, the Lanarkshire Tramway Company initially said that they wished to run tram tracks across it, but by 1929 they had changed their minds. Competition from bus services meant that the company was on its knees, and trams in Motherwell were becoming an endangered species.

This metal arch was built as a prototype for a procession of similar arches that were erected along the Mall in London as part of the celebrations for the coronation of Queen Elizabeth in 1953. Mr T. R. Miller of the Motherwell Bridge company bought the arch for the town and had it re-erected in this location, with the addition of the burgh coat of arms, seen at the centre. Sadly the arch fell into disrepair and had to be dismantled.

The Lanarkshire Tramway Company brought trams to Motherwell in 1903, initially running them from Hamilton to Wishaw. In 1930 the LTC adopted the new name of the Lanarkshire Traction Co., reflecting the increasing pressure it was experiencing from bus operators. All its tram services ceased on 14 February 1931, although it continued to run its own buses for a little longer. In August 1932 it was announced that the LTC was to be acquired by the bus operator Scottish Motor Traction (SMT), which spelled the end for the company. At the time LTC was operating 117 buses. The bus in this 1960s picture was one of a large fleet of Leyland double-deckers operated by Central SMT, and delivered to the company in the late 1940s and early fifties. The photograph was taken in Hamilton Road, with the junction of West Hamilton Street in the right foreground.

Virtually every building and chimney in this picture has been demolished. The street in the foreground is West Hamilton Street, with Brandon Street running behind and parallel to it. Brandon Church, which opened for worship in August 1866, is in the centre of the picture. Tom Johnstone described the church as being of a Gothic design, saying that it formed 'a prominent feature of an otherwise uninteresting streetscape'. I doubt whether he would have found Brandon Parade any more alluring than the Brandon Street it replaced. Although it has an ecclesiastical look about it, the building in the left foreground with the rose window was latterly used as housing. Nancy Riach, the Olympic swimmer, lived in one of the flats it contained. Her father was a police inspector in Motherwell and Nancy died of polio in Monte Carlo in 1947. The single-storey building at the left edge of the picture housed Dan Dunlop's photography business.

All the buildings on the left of this picture of the cross have been demolished. The Motherwell Inn was situated at the centre of the fledgling village, at the corner of Brandon Street and Merry Street. The inn was built in 1820 and was Motherwell's first two-storey building. The prevalence of pubs was a cause of concern to James Clason, who wrote in 1836 that 'There are four public-houses in the parish, which have a most injurious effect upon the morals of the people, and in increasing poverty and disease.' He complained that 'Licenses are too easily obtained'.

THE CROSS, MOTHERWELL

The Motherwell Inn was replaced by the branch of Burton's shown in this picture, and the building is now home to MacDonalds. Tom Johnstone's *Motherwell Memories* is one of the best-known books about old Motherwell, and was published by the Hamilton Advertiser in 1938. It contains a collection of newspaper articles written about the town by Mr Johnstone and published in the *Motherwell Times*. Although he wrote these articles, Tom Johnstone is better-known as a photographer, rather than a journalist.

The church spire in the distance on the left belonged to the former Methodist Church. Methodism was established in Motherwell by incoming English and Welsh workers employed at the Old Malleable. Their first place of worship was at the corner of Milton Street and Roman Road, but following the closure of the old ironworks a more centrally-located church – 'one of the prettiest in the town' – was built in Hamilton Road. The original church was subsequently acquired by Dalziel Co-operative Society and used as a store. One of Motherwell's former passenger railway stations stood adjacent to the library in Hamilton Road. It was opened in February 1871 and came into being when the branch line to Hamilton was built. The current station in Muir Street replaced it, along with the station in Melville Drive (a short street that was accessed from Brandon Street).

Most of these buildings in Muir Street are still standing, although the further part of the two-storey block on the left has been demolished, as has the original station building, beyond it. The station opened on 1 August 1885, and the *Motherwell Times* described it as 'a handsome and every way convenient structure'. The paper did, however, hint that there was some room for improvement: 'It . . . cost the company so much, that a little more expenditure on the booking office would have been neither here nor there, and would have remedied its chief defect.' The Horseshoe Bar still goes by the same name today.

Muir Street looking into Brandon Street. Collins the bakers occupied the shop in the left foreground, while the dental surgery was above it on the first floor. On Saturday 26 December 1891, under the heading 'INCORRIGIBLE BOYS', the *Motherwell Times* reported that William and George Jamieson, sons of a waggon-builder living in Caledonian Street, had been charged with stealing a pair of pigeons from a coal cellar in Muir Street. The boys were aged 11 and 9, and a few weeks previously had been convicted of two other thefts, for which they were sentenced, along with another boy, 'to receive seven stripes with a birch rod'. This time they were given a custodial sentence. In 1836 James Clason was pleased to note that his parishioners were 'in general . . . quiet, sober, industrious, and regular in their conduct. No individual connected with this parish has ever been chargeable with a capital offence, and they have hitherto kept free from any share in intimidation or acts of violence.'

An early view of Merry Street at the cross, with the Motherwell Inn on the right. The low buildings were probably originally thatched, and would have had their tiled roofs and second storey added later. Tom Johnstone writes about similar single-storey cottages on the opposite side of Merry Street, and describes how 'In 1873-74 a number were removed to permit of the erection of Dalziel Parish Church'.

Merry Street, Motherwell.

All the buildings on the left-hand side of this picture of Merry Street have been demolished, although the lower half of the terrace on the right, which begins at the junction with Dalziel Street, has survived relatively unchanged. A private company started producing gas in Motherwell in 1850, and one of its uses was for street-lighting. Gas lamps had to be lit individually each evening by specially employed lamp-lighters, and the lamp standards tended to be quite short, probably because the lamps needed to be accessible. In 1898 Motherwell Town Council made the decision to build an electricity generating station, which opened in February 1901. One of its primary functions was to provide power for electric street lighting, and the light in this picture was probably one of the 'large arc lamps' that the council installed in the town's main streets. A portable maintenance tower, like the one shown here, is visible on the right in the picture on page 17.

MERRY STREET LOOKING WEST, MOTHERWELL

B 3256

Dalziel Parish Church was completed in 1874, then altered and extended in 1897. The bell in the steeple originally served as a town bell, and was rung three times a day, giving Motherwell folk an alarm call at 5.30 in the morning, then sounding at 6 p.m. and again at 10. The institutional-looking building beyond the terrace of tenements on the right was the YWCA, and during the Second World War ration coupons were issued there.

Merry Street, photographed in 1963 following the demolition of the buildings between the YWCA building and Dalziel Parish Church, but prior to pedestrianisation. The windows on the first floor belonged to the lounge bar of the Garrion Hotel, and the area to the left accommodated a ballroom. These buildings are now council offices.

GARRION HOTEL, MOTHERWELL

D 8121

On Friday 24 July 1903 the *Motherwell Times* reported that the town's tram service had begun operating, and on the first day 'From early morning till as late as eleven o'clock at night, the cars ran merrily'. Initial enthusiasm for the new mode of transport had, however, given way to dissatisfaction by the following week. An uncompromising *Times* journalist wrote that 'For incivility to the public, some of the officials employed by the Company will be hard to beat', adding that: 'The cars have not been running a fortnight, yet we could almost fill our columns with instances of insolence, incivility, neglect of duty, and general disregard for the convenience of the public.' A common complaint was drivers failing to allow passengers to get off at their chosen stop.

BRANDON ST. FROM THE CROSS, MOTHERWELL

14884

Brandon Street was entirely demolished to allow the building of Brandon Parade, as this picture, taken from the cross with the Motherwell Inn on the left, illustrates. When the 1859 Ordnance Survey map was drawn up there were barely any buildings on Brandon Street, and a strip of woodland is shown running along a significant length of its south side. By the time of the 1898 survey the street had become completely built up.

THE CROSS, MOTHERWELL.

Motherwell's La Scala cinema opened in 1920 as part of the ABC circuit and survived until 1959. At one point the town had six separate picture houses, but in the early days of cinema locals had to rely on travelling shows. In March 1901 the *Times* reported that Walker's Cinematograph had given cinema performances in the town hall on the previous Monday and Tuesday. The silent films were accompanied by three singers and a pianist, and the paper remarked that: 'The pictures were most realistic and effective, and were viewed with the utmost satisfaction by the audience.' For more on Motherwell's cinemas see *Lanarkshire's Legendary Cinemas* by Bruce Peter, available from Stenlake Publishing.

Like the previous picture, this view looks along Brandon Street towards the cross, but is taken from further back. The only buildings which have survived are the tenements in the distance on the corner of Muir Street and Hamilton Road. The expanse of wall on the right, running along to the cinema, belonged to the goods station that stood behind it. News of the new station was announced in the *Times* in August 1889, when the paper reported that it would almost definitely require 'the removal of all the buildings on the Company's property on the east side of Brandon Street'. This was indeed the case, and many of Motherwell's first-generation buildings were lost in the ensuing demolition. The new wall seems to have been universally loathed. Tom Johnstone described it as 'a monotonous erection' which 'effectively put a closure to any hope of amenity or architectural improvement on that side of Brandon Street', while the Rev. J. B. Jamieson, author of the *Third Statistical Account*, made a plea for the removal of 'the ugly brick wall which separates one side of the main street from the railway goods office and sheds in the heart of the town'.

BRANDON STREET AND ROYAL HOTEL, MOTHERWELL. B.3265.

The prominent frontage of the YMCA is the only surviving landmark in this picture, which looks along Brandon Street towards Windmillhill Street. The Royal Hotel was built in 1873 by James King of Windmillhill House, and the street that ran to the left of it was Melville Drive, where the Caledonian Railway's first passenger station was situated. In 1885 the new Muir Street station made the one in Melville Drive redundant (along with the station next to the library), and 'the street became more or less a backwater'. The building with the pitched roof, to the left of the YMCA, was the Pavilion Cinema, which was built in 1912. Like many early cinemas it also ran variety shows when it first opened. It was demolished in 1966.

The redevelopment of Motherwell town centre began in the early 1960s when the last of the miners rows were demolished and Brandon Parade was built. This picture shows the parade prior to pedestrianisation. Argos currently occupies the Goldberg's site.

Modern houses now stand on the site of these tenements in Mill Road. The children are standing adjacent to the site of the gasworks. During the First World War a row of single-storey houses in front of the gasworks in Merry Street was demolished by a tank to demonstrate the prowess of Britain's newest piece of military technology. The tank was called *Julian*, and toured many towns as part of a campaign to sell War Savings Certificates, one of a number of schemes dreamt up by the government to raise funds for the war.

Demolished tenements on the corner of Dalziel Street and Coursington Road (Coursington Road leads off to the left). Dalziel Co-operative Society was based in this part of the town, and had its main premises in Scott Street (parallel to Coursington Road) and Dalziel Street. The co-op bakery was in Coursington Road, as was its library. In 1911 the society had nearly 7,500 members with twelve shops in the locality. As well as paying a dividend to members on the purchases they made, co-op members benefited from free life insurance. The combination poorhouse for Bothwell, Dalziel, Shotts and Cambusnethan parishes stood in Park Street, at the top of Coursington Road. This was where the destitute were supported by their respective parishes, and according to Tom Johnstone the building was 'drab and prison-like in appearance'. Park Street was used by temperance advocates as an example of the road to rack and ruin because it began with a pub, followed by a pawn-shop, and then finished up with the poorhouse. In 1905 a new poorhouse was built and the old building became the town's second model lodging house (the other one was in Orbiston Street). Model lodging houses provided rented accommodation for working men.

This steam-powered co-op lorry was photographed in Coursington Road, outside what was originally Our Lady of Good Aid Church, now Motherwell Cathedral. The building on the left in the background, built in 1875, was the first chapel in the vicinity, and when the new church was built this became a school. Cathedral Primary School now stands on its site. The writer of this postcard, dated 17 May 1909 and sent to Macduff in Banffshire, talks about sectarian disturbances in Motherwell: 'We have great excitement here just now, perhaps you will see it in some papers, between Catholics and Protestants. I wish it were finished for fear of bloodshed, the feeling is so strong'. An unseemly breach of the peace had its origins in Coursington Road in June 1888. A quarrel broke out between a Motherwell man and a member of a visiting circus, which was performing in a field in front of the street. The man was arrested, but other members of the circus mobbed the police and set him free. When he was rearrested and being taken to the police station, the *Times* reported that '80 or 90 circus men . . . kept constantly stoning the police, and charging them with every description of weapons.' Local people had to be armed with batons by the police to assist them in breaking up the crowd.

The Jerviston Viaduct, dating from 1840, was the first railway viaduct to be built in Scotland. It predated iron girders, and the arches between the stone piers were built entirely from wooden beams. The only metal used took the form of iron sockets that held the beams in place. The viaduct (better-known as the Globe, after the tin-works of the same name that once stood in the vicinity) carried a single-track railway a distance of more than 1,000 feet over the valley of the South Calder Water. At its highest point the line was 110 feet above the ground. Both mineral and passenger traffic used the Wishaw and Coltness Railway, and the viaduct saw fourteen years service, although 'it latterly showed such marked symptoms of its insecurity' that a new bridge and piece of track was built to replace it about a mile away. The new viaduct carried twin tracks and opened in 1857. Its predecessor was taken down in 1922, and the piers were blown up with dynamite, following which the stone was taken to Perthshire and used to build Gleneagles Station and Hotel.

This bridge over the Calder was unsuitable for tram traffic, and when services were extended to New Stevenston, Mossend and Bellshill a new, wider bridge was built adjacent to it. In 1952 the Rev. J. B. Jamieson, author of the *Third Statistical Account*, cited two improvements that Motherwell required, one of which was the cleaning-up of the polluted South Calder Water. It had once been 'a clear-running stream, well stocked with trout', but these were killed in a single night in 1891 after effluent spilled into it from a factory further up the river. The *Motherwell Times* ran a cursory news item on Saturday 9 May 1891 under the heading 'TROUT POISONING', reporting that: 'On Saturday the bed of the River Calder, between Newmains and Motherwell, was thickly covered with trout. The fish, it is supposed, were poisoned by ammonia.' Tom Johnstone recalled that dead fish were 'literally collected in cart loads'.

BOWLING GREENS & TENNIS COURTS, COLVILLE PARK, MOTHERWELL.

91588.JV.

Colvilles gifted the recreation club and park at Jerviston to the company's workers and their families in 1920, and today the facilities are administered by British Steel. Clarke's *Motherwell Directory* of 1896 lists two bowling clubs in the town, Dalziel Bowling Club in Windmillhill Street and Motherwell Bowling Club in Ladywell Road. The golf course in Colville Park was developed as a nine-hole course in the 1920s during the General Strike. Work was carried out by volunteers and was given a boost by the strike, which meant that more people were available to help. There is now a car park in place of the tennis courts in the background of this picture.

Demolished tenements in Parkhead Street, with Camp Street leading uphill to the right. Individual tenement blocks frequently had their own name in addition to the street name, and 'Waverley Terrace' is probably one of these local names. Parkhead Street originally extended across Camp Street as far as Airbles Road, and on the 1912 Ordnance Survey map a clothing factory is marked on the north side of this stretch of the street. Windmillhill Health Centre's car park has taken the place of these substantial-looking tenements.

The location of this Tom Johnstone picture is unknown, but the photograph is likely to have been taken in a local pit, and illustrates the incredibly cramped conditions that miners frequently worked in. The picture is misleading inasmuch as ordinarily miners worked in almost complete darkness, with only the scant light shed by their lamps. Pit ponies were stabled underground and usually had the misfortune to spend their whole lives down the pit; it wasn't practical to transport them up and down the shafts. When ponies were brought above ground they had to have their eyes covered as they couldn't stand the brightness of daylight. If employing ponies down mines seems inhumane, it is worth bearing in mind that before their introduction it was the job of women and children to carry coal from where it was hewn to the surface. In 1842 women, and boys under ten, were prohibited from working underground.

WINDMILLHILL STREET, MOTHERWELL

A.8433

A couple of landmarks have survived and serve to locate this view of Windmillhill Street. The wording 'New Century Bar' is still legible on the gable end of the tenement in the distance, although all the buildings on the left have been demolished, and the Rex has been swept away and replaced by the car park in front of Lidl. Prior to becoming a cinema, The Rex was a theatre called the New Century which staged plays and variety performances. Having been taken over by ABC cinemas, the building was radically remodelled in 1933 when it was partly demolished, re-emerging with a new facade of brown and cream bricks, as seen here. It closed in 1976, had a brief reprieve as an amusement arcade and night club, and was demolished in 1995.

With the exception of the two blocks in the foreground, each containing a shop, all these buildings in Gavin Street have been demolished. A significant proportion of Motherwell's nineteenth century housing stock was tied housing built by employers for incoming workers. Many solid-looking tenements such as these were badly affected by subsidence, while others were razed in the 1940s and fifties because they failed to meet the standards of the time. Rev. Jamieson writes: 'Until municipal houses began to be built, the prevailing type of buildings consisted of a two-storey block of two-roomed (or occasionally three-roomed) houses, the ground floor house entered off the street and the upper flat entered from a stair at the rear. These houses were solidly built, but large numbers of them have been affected to a greater or lesser extent by underground workings. Very few of these houses have indoor sanitation.'

Tinkers Lane, Motherwell.

Tinkers' Lane, with part of the old tramway depot, known as the Power Station, on the extreme left, and the buildings of what was originally called Airbles House in the centre. This was built as a poorhouse and hospital, replacing the more Dickensian establishment in Park Street and opening in 1905. There was a craze for roller-skating during the early twentieth century, and a skating rink, marked on the 1912 Ordnance Survey map, stood adjacent to the Power Station. This was latterly annexed by the Lanarkshire Tramway Company and used by them as a bus garage, although it was subsequently gutted by fire.

This Orange walk was photographed in Caledonian Street (now Bellshill Road), where B&Q is now situated. The houses on the right were built by the Caledonian Railway Company for their workers, and were known as the 'Caley Blocks'. The picture features on a postcard which was sent in November 1910, some months after the marching season. There was an Orange walk in Motherwell on Sunday 3 July that year, and the participants assembled at the Masonic hall in Hope Street before marching along Muir Street, Brandon Street and Windmillhill Street to South Dalziel Parish Church. The year's principal walk took place the following Sunday in Glasgow when the various lodges affiliated with Motherwell marched from Kelvingrove Park to Scotstoun. A number of skirmishes were reported, as frequently attended these controversial marches.

An unrecognisable view of Fern Street. The new Benefits Agency offices stand on the site of these three substantial villas, one of which was the manse for the Clason Church. Taggarts garage and showroom occupies most of the land on the near side of the road. Quarrying was originally a much more important commercial enterprise in Motherwell than either coal-mining or iron- and steel-making. In 1836 it was recorded that: 'At the Windmill-hill quarry, at present wrought in two places, a very hard rough-grained freestone . . . is much sought after by masons, for forming chimney heads, and also by the proprietors of iron forges, for pavement, &c. it having been ascertained to be unequalled for standing both the weather and the fire. It was of this strong and durable stone that the bridge near Hamilton was built.' Tom Johnstone refers to one Thomas King, 'quarrymaster', who lived in Windmillhill House.

FLEMINGTON STATION, BY MOTHERWELL.

Flemington station opened in March 1901 in what had become a highly industrialised part of Motherwell. The *Times* reported that: 'Owing to the large number of public works in the vicinity of the station it will be a great boon, as previously would-be railway passengers had to travel to Motherwell, a distance of fully half-a-mile.' The station closed to passenger traffic on 4 January 1965.

The Lanarkshire
Steel Co. Ltd
Bricklayers
23/10/07

In March 1891 directors of the Lanarkshire Steel Company and their guests assembled at the company's new works in Flemington to see the first ingot being cast. The works were built to produce 'all classes of angles and bars for ship and bridge building and general engineering purposes' and initially consisted of a bar mill and guide mill. The *Times* reported that 'a large plate mill of the most modern construction' was likely to be installed, and noted that as fifty acres of land had been feued for the works they would undoubtedly end up being very sizeable. Bricklayers such as these were employed to reline blast furnaces. Because of the intense heat, the brickwork within the furnaces had a relatively short lifespan and needed to be repaired or replaced regularly. Much of the work was done on Sundays when the furnaces weren't lit, but this was still a notoriously hot and unpleasant job.

Shields Glen was presented to Motherwell by the Hamiltons of Dalzell in 1906. Donating public parks was a favourite gesture of Victorian industrialists, but often their generosity was at odds with their business interests. On 28 December 1889 the *Motherwell Times* reported that: 'Considerable anxiety and indignation have been caused during the year by the decision of the Duke of Hamilton [a member of a different branch of the Hamilton family] to work out the coal beneath much of the most valuable property in the town. The unfortunate feuars have remonstrated in vain, and already considerable damage has been done to house property'. Such practices were not unusual, and subsidence caused widespread damage to buildings in Motherwell. Shields Glen is no longer meticulously-tended and planted with shrubs and flowers, but still exists, more as a small area of wilderness than a park. There used to be a house in the glen occupied by the gardener, Mr MacDonald. Like the tenements in Range Road on the right of this picture, it no longer exists.

It isn't clear whether this Tom Johnstone photograph was posed, or really features a homeless child. Churches were originally responsible for the poor of their parish, and supported them using money from Sunday collections. There was a strong stigma attached to being 'on the parish', and only the most desperate sought help – or were given it. In 1845 care of the poor was formalised, with the appointment of inspectors of the poor and the obligation to provide poorhouses. Local taxes could be levied where necessary to pay for this. Motherwell's original poorhouse in Park Street was replaced by Airbles House, which opened in 1905 and also served as a hospital. The building was marked 'Poorhouse' on the 1912 map, but had acquired the more politically-correct title of 'Airbles House Public Assistance Institution' by 1939. In 1792 Robert Clason recorded that there wasn't a single person in his parish 'having recourse to the degrading practice of begging'.

The firm of Anderson, Boyes & Co. was established at Flemington in 1899. The company made electric coal-cutting and transporting equipment, and was founded by Alexander Anderson of Law and Thomas Boyes of Carluke. They sold their first piece of coal-cutting machinery to the Summerlee Iron Co. in 1900. The company closed in the 1990s.

Newarthill Road, Carfin, looking towards Motherwell. At the beginning of the twentieth century Orr, Watt & Co. established an engineering works adjacent to Carfin station. The works closed in the 1930s, and the premises were taken over by British National Electrics Ltd. They made domestic electrical goods such as kettles and irons. Coal was wrought on a large scale in Carfin and Newarthill at a much earlier date than it was in Motherwell. In November 1820 the Carfin Colliery appeared to be benefiting from the introduction of new technology, when it stated that 'by the Powers of a Steam Engine, the Splint Coal is now in full working order at the above colliery, and a regular supply may be depended upon'. It went on to add that 'the quality of this Seam of Coal is so well known as to require no commendation'. The blast furnaces of Old Monkland were heavily dependent on supplies of splint coal, which were transported to them from collieries such as the one at Carfin by the Wishaw and Coltness Railway. Incidentally, the steam engine referred to would probably have been used to pump water out of the pit, rather than for traction. Water in underground workings was a major problem and often prevented coal from being reached. Devices on the surface called horse-gins were used for haulage. A horse was harnessed to a long beam connected to some sort of winching device. The horse walked round in a circle, turning the beam, and operating the winch.

Carfin Road, Newarthill, looking east. The contractor Robert McAlpine was born in Newarthill in 1847, and at the age of ten became a trapper at Newarthill Colliery. This involved working on the surface alongside the winding engineman, opening and shutting the cage doors to release full coal hutches as they were brought to the surface, and shunt empty ones back. McAlpine subsequently became a miner, and having left the village with his family after his father died and his mother remarried, took a weekend bricklaying job to supplement his full-time occupation. He gradually built up the construction company that still bears his name today. In 1879, while still a small concern, the company built the station buildings at Carfin. In later life McAlpine earned the nickname of 'Concrete Bob' for his enthusiasm for this building material. McAlpine's built the Glenfinnan Viaduct, the first concrete viaduct in Britain, and an important piece of civil engineering.

Gutty Square was the name given to the two-storey tenement block on the far corner of Mosshall Street and the area behind it. It apparently got its name because children used to play around the back in their gutties. James Muir's bakers shop stood on the near corner of Mosshall Street, although the white single-storey building with a thatched roof shown in this picture possibly predated the sandstone bakery building. The gable end with the word 'BAR' on it belonged to the White House, originally a free house owned by a Mrs McIntyre. This was latterly called the Gordon Arms, and was destroyed by a fire in the 1970s.

A closer view of Gutty Square, which like the single-storey cottages beyond it has been demolished. The stripy pole marked the premises of Jake the barber, whose shop was later taken over by Mr Burton's shoe repair business. The Cross Keys Tavern closed in the late 1920s after which it was used as a doctor's surgery. Newarthill is in Bothwell Parish, and in 1836 Matthew Gardiner wrote of his parishioners that 'The agricultural part of the population are sober, active, and intelligent'. He went on to describe handloom weavers as 'sadly depressed in their circumstances' following the introduction of powerlooms, concluding rather ambiguously that 'The colliers and miners exhibit the usual characteristics of these classes', although it's not clear whether this was a slur or not. The 1859 OS map shows Newarthill as quite an extensive settlement, with at least four coal and ironstone pits in the vicinity and about a dozen sites marked as 'old pit'. Matthew Gardiner made the wild prediction that coal reserves in Bothwell Parish were so great that its collieries would be able to sustain 'an annual output of 400,000 tons for upwards of 3000 years'.

The previous two pictures look east along High Street towards Newhouse; this one was taken from the opposite direction, looking back towards Gutty Square which is on the left. In an article about Newarthill included in *Motherwell Memories*, Tom Johnstone refers to the village's oldest inhabitant, 95-year-old 'Granny' Dempster, noting that 'Although resident in the village for over fifty years she is still regarded as an incomer by the rather conservative natives'!

Church Street, Newarthill. There is some confusion as to whether the two buildings on the near side of the church were both pubs. The further-away one may have been McCaskie's bar, which then became the Wheel and was incorporated into the present-day Brannock Inn. The white terrace in the foreground is believed to have been Wee Lizzie's pub. These weren't the only local pubs, and for a relatively small village Newarthill was well-stocked with places to buy a drink. The church in this picture was built in 1802 and changed hands between a bewildering variety of sects, including Anti-Burghers and members of the United Secession and United Presbyterian churches.

With the possible exception of the one on the right, all these cottages in High Street, looking towards Newhouse, have been demolished. The coal seams in the north and east of Bothwell Parish lie relatively near the surface, which is why coal was mined on a large scale in Newarthill and Carfin earlier than in some of the other nearby mining communities. Newarthill quickly became quite substantial, and in 1836 was described as one of the 'principal villages' of Bothwell Parish. Of the three schools in the parish, the one at Holytown only had about 20 pupils, compared to more than 100 at Newarthill.

A description of the buildings in the village set out in *The Newarthill Story* includes mention of 'the red sandstone row of houses which housed the yard of Robertsons Fruit Merchants', going on to say that 'next to this property [stood] probably the largest house in Newarthill, built by James Scobbie, a one time leading contractor in the collieries'. The sender of this postcard, postmarked Newarthill and posted in 1913, suggests that these are the same red sandstone houses, writing that the path on the left, behind the children, 'leads into a coalmasters house standing in its own grounds'. The terrace in the picture has survived relatively unchanged, with only the addition of dormer windows and the removal of the iron railings. The houses are numbered 407-413 High Street.